THE camera book

loads of things you can do with a camera

john davis

Frances Lincoln Ltd
74–77 White Lion Street
London N1 9PF
www.franceslincoln.com

The Camera Book
Copyright © Frances Lincoln 2015

First Frances Lincoln edition 2015

John Davis has asserted his right to be identified
as the author of this work in accordance with the
Copyright, Designs and Patents Act 1988 (UK).

A catalogue record for this book is available from the
British Library.

ISBN 978-0-7112-3644-8

Printed and bound in China

9 8 7 6 5 4 3 2 1

Please note that any reader or anyone in their charge
taking part in any of the activities described in this
book does so at their own risk. Neither the author
nor the publisher can accept any legal responsibility
for any harm, injury, damage, loss or prosecution
resulting from the use or misuse of the activities,
techniques, tools and advice in the book.

contents

discovering cameras

The first time I picked up a camera and took a few shots, I was hooked. The world around me suddenly looked different – it felt like I could see all sorts of things that I had never noticed before. I took pictures of my family, and noticed lots of new things about them – dad's face crinkled up when he smiled, and mum's hair looked amazing close up. I started to take pictures of my family and friends outdoors and indoors, at night and during the day. Then I experimented with the buildings and landscape around me, taking distant and close-up shots. It felt like the world was revealing itself in a new and exciting way – and that's what I hope these projects will do for you.

You can start the book at the beginning and do the projects one after another, or you can dip straight in to any one that sounds exciting and do that. There are photo projects for indoors and outdoors, because moving between these two will really help you notice the difference that light makes to a photo. Outdoors, natural sunlight can act like a beam

Cameras are really safe to play with, but there are a few things to bear in mind when you are taking photographs.

- Always stand still when taking a photo. Never try to take a photo while you are walking, because you may trip or stumble.

- When you are photographing outside, never point your camera into the sun, or look at it directly. The sun provides brilliant lighting for photos, but it can hurt your eyes if you look at it directly or through the camera's viewfinder.

- Do not use your camera underwater unless it has been designed especially to do this. Cameras do not like getting wet!

- If your camera stops working properly, ask an adult for help. Do not try to take it apart yourself, even to change a battery. The electronic parts inside a camera can sometimes cause an electric shock.

- If your camera feels hot or malfunctions in any way, turn it off and ask an adult for help.

shining down between trees, for instance, or bathe your whole photo in light. Indoors, you will probably want to start playing with directing light towards your subjects, and even using simple reflector boards (see page 42).

Shadows are just as important as light, because they make strong shapes on photos. They are great for trick photography too – you can give a shadow a bunch of flowers, for instance (see page 96). When you're playing with light and shadow, you will also begin to notice what fun you can have with reflection. I've included a few projects that use reflection to create interesting effects (such as the sunglasses project on page 51).

With this book and a camera in your hands, you will find out how to take brilliant pictures of people and objects. We've made it easy to decide which projects to do by labelling them with stars to indicate their level of difficulty. Projects with one star ❄ can be done by children of almost any age; those with two stars ❄❄ can be done by children of five or older, but younger children may require adult help; while three-star projects ❄❄❄ are more suitable for children aged eight or more.

You can take photographs in your bedroom, in the garden, in the park, on holiday, or out with your friends or family. And the best thing is, they'll last forever.

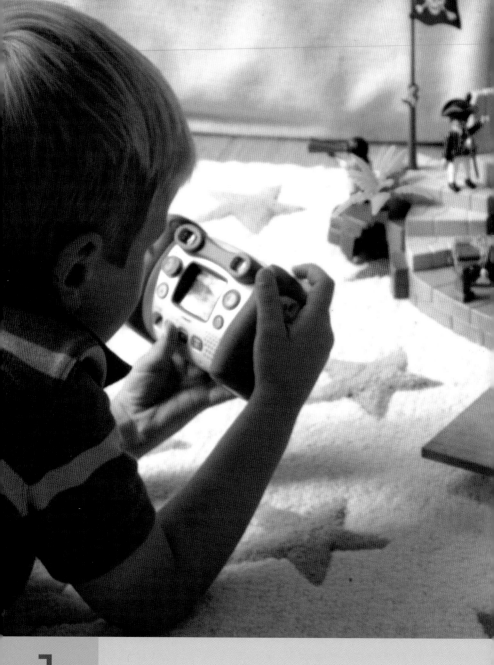

1

indoor shots

01 create a still life

A 'still life' is a picture of objects arranged in a particular way, like some fruit in a bowl. Try setting up a fruit bowl near a window and photographing it without using your flash, to experiment with natural light.

- Ask your parents if you can borrow some interesting fruits or vegetables that you would like to photograph. Pick as many different colours and shapes as you can.

- Arrange them in a fruit bowl so that the bowl looks full and overflowing, then place the bowl on a table near a window. Make sure you don't have too many distractions in the background.

- Try shooting from several angles, and changing the background by hanging some material up behind the fruit.

focus on one thing

✳✳

For this project you also need a collection of objects, such as a vase of flowers, but now you're going to focus on just one thing. This project is great for understanding one of the special functions on your camera.

Find the close-up mode on your camera (it looks like this: ❀). This will allow you to get really close to one flower and make the other flowers go out of focus. If your camera doesn't have a close-up mode, use the zoom to get close to the flower. If you are using the camera on your mobile phone, tap the screen where you want the camera to focus and it will hone in on the single flower, making the other flowers go out of focus.

Fill the frame with all the flowers so you have a photograph that is full of colour.

photograph your bedroom

Your bedroom is probably full of your favourite things. Take a photograph of them all together – you'll be surprised at how much it feels like 'you'.

● Go to your bedroom and get out all the things that you love. Choose things that you think show what kind of person you are and what you like to do.

● Arrange them in your bedroom so that you can see them all in the camera, then choose the best angle to get them all in. Have a point of interest in the photograph such as your favourite toy or something that shows your favourite hobby.

● Use the daylight from your window to light the objects.

Walk around the room and stop to look through your camera now and then. Where is the best place to stand, to get a really interesting photograph?

04

one object, five ways

This is a great way to experiment with shapes. Find a colourful object and ask yourself, 'How can I photograph this in a different way?'

● Pick a colourful object from anywhere in your home and put it on a plain background, such as a table top or the floor, so nothing else will be a distraction in your photograph.

● Look at the settings on your camera and find the close-up setting, which will look like this: ❀. This setting means you can go in really close to your object but keep it in focus.

● Set your camera to close-up mode, then stand or kneel really close to the object. Photograph different sections of the object – such as the handle. Do not show the whole object in one shot.

● Try taking photographs from lots of different angles, with and without using the close-up mode.

create a flicker book

This is a fun way to create your own animated film using 'stop motion'. You do this by photographing the same object in the same way, from the same place, lots of times over the course of a week, a month or even a year.

● Set up a vase of fresh flowers in a place that they can stay, untouched, for at least a week. Decide where to stand to take your photograph, and mark your position somehow. (Chalk is good, but check with your parents before marking anything.)

● Photograph the flowers every day for a week or more. Then print all your photos and put them together in order, starting with your first shot. Staple the photos together on the left-hand side so you create a book. Now flick through the book and watch how the flowers start wilting in front of your eyes.

06

shoot the outside, inside!

In this project you can be a real wildlife photographer from the comfort of your own bedroom.

● Look out of a bedroom window and see what kinds of places birds and wildlife (like squirrels) land. Then go outside and place some food like seeds or nuts in those places.

● Get in position by the window, with your camera, and take some test shots so you know you will be ready once something starts eating your food.

● Use the zoom function on your camera to get as close as possible to the wildlife that arrives.

Try putting the torch in different positions to see all the different shadows it creates and how many spooky faces you can get.

spooky face pictures

Usually we use the sun or camera flash for lighting, but you can get some spooky pictures using a torch.

● You will need a torch and the help of a friend or one of the family for this project.

● Turn off the flash on your camera.

● Put your camera on something solid, so it won't move during the shot and give you a blurry photograph.

● Ask your friend to switch on a torch and hold it under his or her chin, then stay very still. Turn the lights off in the room so the torch is the only light. Then take some photographs. Notice how the shadows make someone look really spooky!

guess the object

**

Some ordinary household objects look very strange if you photograph one part, very close up. If you give your friends just one photo, can they guess the object?

● Choose an everyday object in your home that you think would be fun to photograph. Put it on a plain piece of paper or card so that there are no distractions in the background

● Find the close-up mode on your camera, which is shown by this symbol ❁. Move around your object – try turning it around or upside down, so that when you look through the camera even you can't work out what you are looking at. Take a few shots, then pick the strangest one to give to your friends and ask them to guess what it is.

Remember to photograph the whole object as well, so that you can show your friends what the object was if they can't guess it.

09 shoot your dinner

This is your chance to be a top food photographer by photographing your dinner being prepared and cooked.

- On a day when you are at home, ask if you can take photographs of your dinner being prepared.

- Photograph the ingredients when they are chopped and prepared, but still raw.

- Once your food is cooked, ask if you can help putting it onto a plate or bowl, so you can arrange the food in a way that you think would make a good photograph. Make sure you can see all the different types of food.

- Stand over the bowl or plate and photograph your dinner from above, like they do in cook books and magazines.

experiment with colour

Choose one of your most colourful toys, and then find a background in a very different colour. The contrast in colours will really make your toy stand out in the photo.

The background for your photo could be a piece of coloured material, coloured paper or even a coloured piece of clothing. The colours with the most contrast are green against red, purple against yellow and blue against orange. When you are next outside, look at the colours of flowers and plants – which two colours look really good together?

11

✳✳ set up a mini film set

Why not spend an afternoon being a film director? Your toys can be the cast, and you can take lots of pictures to tell a story, moving the toys between each shot.

Make up a story for your toys: your pirates could be searching for buried treasure, or your teddy bears could be having a teddy bears' picnic. Set up the first scene with your toys, take a picture, then move them and shoot again. You'll probably be surprised at how long your story gets!

2 animals

and pets

12

* zoos and farmyards

Animals are fun to photograph, especially when they are relaxed and behaving naturally, so make sure you have a camera with you next time you go to a zoo or farm.

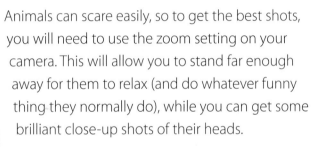

Animals can scare easily, so to get the best shots, you will need to use the zoom setting on your camera. This will allow you to stand far enough away for them to relax (and do whatever funny thing they normally do), while you can get some brilliant close-up shots of their heads.

If you don't have a zoom, find a good place to stand to get some group shots, or whole-body shots. If it's a sunny day, wait until the animals walk into the sunlight. Don't use a flash, because this can hurt animals' eyes.

Be patient and keep looking through the camera; you might have to wait, at the ready, for several minutes for that perfect shot.

capture stillness

Animals are very still and focused when they look out of a window onto the natural world, and you can get a great picture by taking a photograph from outside.

If you have a pet, take your camera with you for the next few times that you go out into the garden. Look back towards the house – one day, you're likely to see your pet staring out of a window. Compose your photograph so that the window frame acts like a picture frame for your pet, and use the zoom on your camera so you don't frighten your pet and cause it to run away.

picture a dog running

Find out how to use a panning technique – like they do in the movies – by photographing a dog running.

● 'Panning' is where you take a photograph while keeping the camera on a moving object, such as a dog – so your arms move to allow the camera to stay focused on the dog. The end result will show the dog in focus and the background blurred and out of focus, which gives the sensation of speed.

● If you or your friends have a dog, take it to the park and ask your friend to throw a stick for it so you can photograph it running. If you don't have a dog, visit a park where dogs (or people!) run about, and practise the technique on them.

Once you have mastered the art of panning, you can photograph your friends running, swimming, riding their bikes, whizzing by on skateboards, or any other kind of fast activity.

photograph a pet trick

✳✳

This project takes a bit of pre-planning, because you need to teach your pet a trick and find a great place to take the perfect photograph.

● First, you'll need to teach your pet a trick. The easiest trick to do is to hold some food in the air, just above your pet's reach, so it will stretch up towards the food. Try this trick at home before you go on location, so your pet already knows what you want it to do.

● Then choose a location where there won't be too many distractions, so your dog (or cat!) will focus on you. Remember to take along some food treats too, for use in the trick.

● When you are ready to take the photograph, lie on the ground near your pet, to get a more dramatic photograph. Ask a friend to hold the food treat in the air above your pet.

● Look through your camera and be prepared to start taking pictures immediately, because animals can be unpredictable and you don't want to miss the funniest shot.

16

be an underwater photographer

Deep-sea divers take photographs of fish while they are underwater, but you can do this on dry land if you or your friends have some fish in a tank.

You will need to be able to photograph around a fish tank for this project. The idea is to get as close to the fish as possible, and take photographs that don't show the edge of the tank. You want it to look as though perhaps the fish were swimming in the big, open sea, and you might have been swimming with them. Try to focus on the fish, and make sure your flash is turned off, because if your camera flashes, it will make a flare reflection on the glass, which will look like a white blob in your photo.

17

* zoom up on a pet!

You can get some amazing photographs if you take really close-up shots of an animal. Zoom in to see all the details in a way you've never seen them before.

Whether you're at home or on safari, you need to be very patient when photographing animals. This is because they need time to get used to you being there and because you might have to wait a while for the perfect shot. Get down onto the same level as your pet and sneak up to it quietly. Get as close to it as you can, and use the zoom ⊕⊖ setting if you have one. Try to make the animal's face fill the frame.

see like an animal

Pretend that you are a pet animal in a cage and take a photograph from the animal's perspective.

✳✳

● To take a photo that shows what your pet sees, you will need to hold the camera close to the floor of the cage. Make sure the shot includes some of the things in the cage, such as the water bottle, food dish, bedding and any bars on the cage.

● If it is a small cage and you find it difficult to take the photograph while holding the camera, put the camera on the self-timer mode ☉ to take the photograph.

● Experiment with different angles and points of interest.

19

** wildlife lucky dip

Go into the woods or your local park and photograph all the birds and wild animals that you see. You will probably be surprised at the wildlife you find.

Next time you visit a park or wood, take your camera. Find a position where you think you might see some local wildlife, and stand very still – you will need to wait for a few minutes for any wildlife to appear. Remember to look up into the trees, around on bushes and branches, and down to the ground. Use your zoom for close-up shots, but always take a distance shot first, in case the noise of the zoom frightens the animal away.

3   people

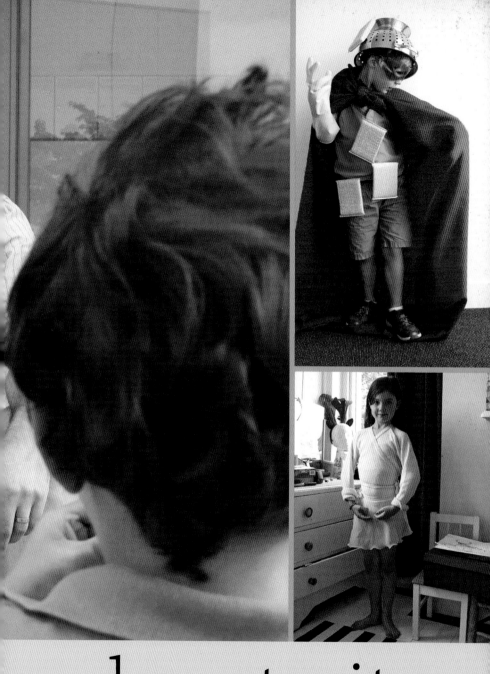

and portraits

20

**

use reflector boards

This project will show you how you can change the light for your photograph by using different reflectors, which are just large pieces of coloured card, paper or fabric.

- You will need two friends to experiment with reflector boards.

- Ask one friend to stand next to a window, so the window is to the side of her. Take a photo just using the light coming in from the window (my photo like this is shown opposite, top left).

- Now ask a friend (or parent) to hold a large piece of white card very close to your first friend's face, while standing opposite the window. The white card will reflect the light from the window back into your friend's face. Take a photo (my photo like this is shown opposite, top right).

- Swap the white card with a black card. This will have the opposite effect to the white card: it will make the shadow stronger on one side of her face. Take a photo or two (my photo is shown opposite, bottom left).

- Experiment with silver foil on card too!

21

take a family portrait

Photograph your family in front of your home. This is a great shot to take each year and stick in a family history scrapbook, along with other souvenirs.

● Ask your whole family to sit in front of the main doorway. This will give you a great background and frame the photograph well.

● Tell everyone where they should stand. The difficult part of shooting a family portrait is getting everyone's eyes open and looking in the same direction at the same time, so you will need to let everyone know when you are going to take the photograph. Shout really loudly: 'OK everyone, look at me and smile!'

a year of 'selfies'

This is a fun way to document your year. Photograph yourself once a week, in 'selfies', for a whole year and see how much you change.

● This project is most easily done using the camera on your phone, but you can also use a camera with a timer function.

● Decide on a location and background that you can use all year, such as a wall in your bedroom, and try to take the same position for most photographs. This makes it easy to compare all the shots at the end of the year. Prepare to be surprised at the results!

23

use your flash at night

You can create a striking portrait outside at night by using the flash on your camera.

● Fill your frame with your subjects, by standing so close to them that you cannot see very much of the background.

● Turn on your camera flash. When the flash goes off, it will be very close to your subjects, so it will really light up their faces.

● The background of your picture will stay very dark, helping to make the people – and especially their faces – stand out.

● Another way to take a portrait at night is to use the night portrait mode on your camera: ☾. This will allow natural light to come into the photograph, such as the glow of a sunset.

take portraits of your friends

Get a group of your friends together and photograph each of them showing their personalities. Ask them to dress up in a way that shows their hobbies or other things they like, and choose locations that seem just right for that person. If you have a friend who plays a lot of sport, for instance, ask them to put on their favourite sports kit. If they play a musical instrument, photograph them playing it.

25

fill the gap

In this project, you will take a photo of your friends and be in the photo too, by using the self-timer button ⟳ on your camera.

● When you use the timer button on your camera, you usually have about 10 seconds before the camera takes a photo, so you need to plan the picture carefully. Ask your friends to stand in a group (posing them in fun ways, if you like) and make sure they have left a gap for you to join the group.

● Put the camera in position and set the self-timer. Walk quickly over to your friends and get in position for the shot. You will hear a few beeps from the camera – this is like a countdown for the last few seconds before it takes the photo – and then you will see a light flash. If you're in position, you're in the shot!

26 run, jump, snap

This is a great way to take an action 'selfie' – the trick is in the timing, and you might need a few practice shots.

● Choose the location and background that you want. Find somewhere solid to place the camera, such as a table or bench, and check through the viewfinder that the camera is lined up on the right spot and the background looks good.

● When you are ready, set the camera to the self-timer mode – ○ – and run around to where you want to be photographed.

● Watch out for the flashing light, which will tell you that you have 10 seconds before the camera takes the picture. Count down from 10 and try to jump just as the shutter clicks.

sunglass reflections

This is a different and fun way to photograph a landscape, by finding it on a pair of glasses.

● Find an interesting-looking landscape – this might be buildings, fields, a wood, river or mountains.

● On a sunny day, ask a friend or family member to put on some sunglasses or goggles and to look at the view you want to photograph. Move around the person so that you can see the different ways that the landscape is reflected in their glasses.

● Put your camera onto close-up mode (❀) if you have this, so you can get very close but keep your photo in focus.

● Take a series of photos and see how many different views you can get. Take some photos that show you in the reflection.

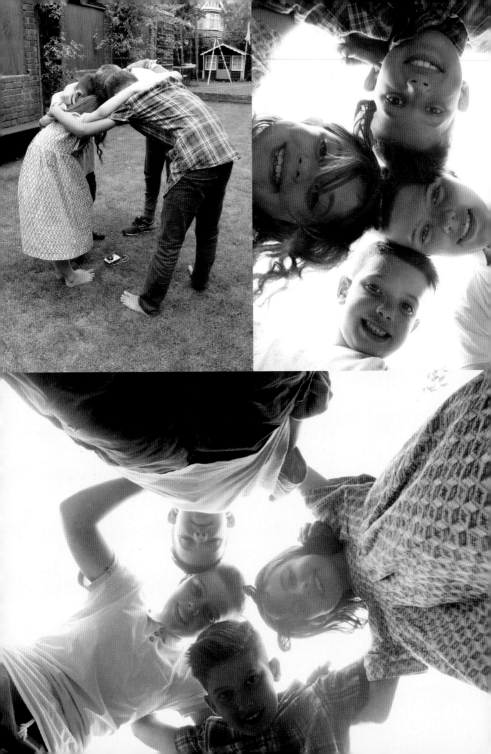

take an up-shot group shot

This is a great way to photograph you and your friends all together. The photographs can be done anywhere, because it doesn't really matter what the background is.

● To take an up-shot photo, you will need to find the self-timer button on your camera, which will look like this: ○

● Gather your friends around in a circle. Press the self-timer button on the camera to activate it, then place it on the ground in the middle of your friendly circle and rejoin your friends. Make sure you are all looking down over the camera, making silly faces or smiling and laughing as you all wait for the camera to go off. Try taking lots of pictures pulling different faces.

Try an up-shot at night with the flash turned on too – your faces will appear out of nowhere!

29

guess what I do?

Take a photo of your mum, dad or another adult with props that show what they do for a job. Then ask your friends to 'guess the job' in every photo.

● Think about what your mum or dad do for a job and collect some props to illustrate what they do.

● Ask them to wear something that shows what they do and then ask them to stand in a place that also provides a clue. Take a few shots and choose the best one for the guessing game.

It looks like this dad might be a gardener. What are the things that provide the clues?

create a superhero

✱✱

Let your imagination go wild with this project and make your friends look like superheroes.

Ask your parents if you can use some household props to make a friend or sibling look like a superhero. Everyday kitchen utensils can become earth-saving weapons: colanders make good space helmets, washing-up gloves could protect superhero hands, and tea towels (or blankets) can be transformed into magic capes that could help someone fly through the galaxy. Look in the bathroom and bedrooms too: rubber bath mats could armour someone from alien attack and eye patches and masks are great for hiding someone's true identity. Then dress up your friends or siblings and ask them to pose in superhero poses while you take lots of photos.

4 outdoor

shots

31

find the alphabet

If you look all around you, you will begin to see that there are letters of the alphabet in all sorts of unlikely places. Try to find all 26 letters of the alphabet.

When you're outside, look up, down, left and right for letters of the alphabet that crop up in nature or everyday objects. Try the wheel of a bike for the letter O, or the bough of a tree for the letter V. You will be surprised at what you find and what you would normally miss. Remember to check what is in your viewfinder, and move close enough to make the letter fill the frame. After doing this, you'll find you are looking at everything in a completely different way.

Your toys could be hiding all sorts of letters. Hold your camera close up over various parts to find them!

32

* choose a colour

This is a great project to do on a walk. Choose a colour – such as blue – then look out for things that have lots of that colour in them. Take close-up and distance shots.

Before you go for a walk, choose a colour or ask one of your friends to give you a colour. As you are walking, look out for that colour; remember that it may feature as just part of an object or the whole thing. You may be surprised at how often your chosen colour turns up!

33

play with the sun

This project will help you understand what effect sunlight has on objects, depending on whether it is in front, behind, or to the side of objects.

● Go into the garden or park with a ball (a football is a good size) and place it on the ground.

● Move around the ball and photograph it from different sides. Notice that when the sun lights up one side of the ball, there is a shadow on the other side of the ball and on the ground.

● See how many photographs you can take of the ball with different shadows.

You could also try photographing the ball from the same place at different times of day to see how the sunlight changes.

people and sunlight

Sometimes you'll want photos of people to be evenly lit, and other times you might want to add a blaze of sunlight. Here are some ways to experiment.

● Ask some friends or siblings to stand in front of you with the sun behind you. Having the sun behind the camera will make the colours in your photo become stronger and more intense.

● Now move so that the sun is in front of you (behind your friends) and take a photograph of a scene with the sun in front of you. Notice that in this photo, the colours are washed out and the photo has a kind of a hazy look – this is caused by light flaring into your lens. If you want, you can reduce this by putting your hand above the lens and blocking out the sunlight. Do not look at the sun; focus only on your friends.

***

take the car to bits

This is a fun way to make a photographic jigsaw puzzle.
Take pictures of an object, zooming in so you just shoot
one section at a time, then put all the photos together.

● A car makes a good subject for this puzzle. You need to move around the car, taking pictures of sections of it quite close up. Always stand on the pavement and use your zoom, so that you are safe, and only do this in the company of an adult.

● Photograph the front headlights, front wheel, bonnet, wing mirrors, front door, roof, back door, boot, and the rear lights and wheel.

● Make prints of your photos and ask your friends if they can assemble them into a picture of a car.

36

where was I?

This is a fun game to play with your friends, where they have to guess where you have been on a walk by looking at your photographs and working it out.

- Photograph your walk to school or your walk to the park and take pictures of all the interesting things that you see on the way. Start taking your photographs as soon as you leave home, and look out for unusual things on the way, such as a colourful gate, a funny mark on a wall, or an interesting door.

- Take pictures all along your route, and then finish with an abstract photograph of the end point (which might be something like your school entrance or the big gates to the park).

- Think really hard how you can make your photographs a little bit puzzling, so your friends don't guess immediately what they are looking at. Try different angles and use the zoom to come in really close to things. Then show your friends your series of pictures and see if they can guess where you have been.

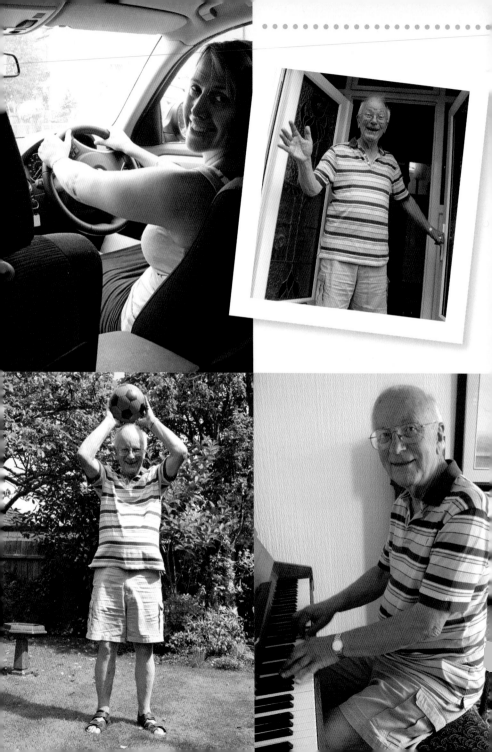

create a picture diary

Newspaper photographers try to tell a story with pictures, and you can too. Pick a day that you think will be interesting, and take photographs at different points during the day to build a picture-story of the people you saw and the things you did.

● Remember that every story has a beginning, a middle and an end, so start photographing soon after you wake up, to create 'the beginning'. You might want to start by snapping an interesting breakfast or part of a car journey. It's up to you to decide where the story starts.

● Once you have arrived at your destination (which might be grandma and grandpa's house, or the local swimming pool or park) take photographs of where you are and who else is there. Try to show lots of things that happen during the day (even funny little things, like grandpa going to sleep in a chair). Then photograph your journey home. The next day, put your photos into story order.

38

** make a shadow person

This project shows you how to photograph a shadow person with a funny face.

● Find a flat area where you can make a shadow, such as a playground or beach. Remember that you need to stand with the sun behind you to make a shadow.

● Make up a funny face by using objects you can find nearby, such as pebbles for eyes, leaves or seaweed for hair, and twigs for a mouth and nose. When you are happy with your face, ask a friend to stand so that their head-shadow falls over the face.

● Direct them to do some funny shapes with their arms as well so the shadow comes to life. Remember not to get your own shadow in the photograph.

39

** photograph a mini-beast

Go out into the garden or park and look for mini-beasts under leaves and bits of bark or wood. Look closely at spider webs too: they often have amazing creepy crawlies caught in or patrolling the web.

● In this project, you will photograph a mini-beast really close up, so you can see all the details of its intricate body.

● To make sure you can photograph close up and in focus, you will need to set your camera to the close-up setting: 🌷. If you have a phone or digital music player that has a camera, try using this even though it won't have the icon – you can still get great pictures sometimes. Make sure you hold your camera really still or rest it on something so you don't get blurred photos.

40

find the best view

This is like being a landscape painter, but using a camera to make an amazing picture of the great outdoors.

When you find somewhere you want to photograph, try standing in several different positions and kneeling down or getting higher to take the shot. Look for a point of interest to include at one side of the photograph, so that when someone looks at the picture, their eyes will be drawn into and around the photograph. If you can, pick the best time of day, too, for the kind of light you want to capture. If you have a landscape option 🖾 on your camera, use this to keep everything in focus.

do some fire writing

Photographing someone 'writing' with a sparkler needs some special techniques. You will also need a few sparklers and the help of an adult and a friend.

● Photographs taken at night need a long exposure, so you will need to get your camera ready before you start. Look for a 'B' setting or a night-time setting on your camera. If you don't have these, make sure your flash is turned off.

● Because the exposure will be 2–10 seconds long, the camera will have to sit on a tripod, wall, or level surface to hold it absolutely still, otherwise you will get blurred photographs.

● Ask an adult to light the sparkler, then get ready to take the photograph. Give your friend a count-down (say "3–2–1") so he or she knows when to start writing in the air.

● If you don't have any sparklers, try using a torch to do the writing. This also works really well and doesn't need adult help.

42

catch a blazing sky

You can get some beautiful photographs when you photograph a sunset – the colours in the sky become really rich and your photograph will be glowing.

● The most important point to remember when you take pictures of the sky during sunset is to turn off your flash. This is because you are photographing light, and you don't want a different kind of light (like a camera flash) to interfere with the multi-coloured light in the sky.

● Because you are not using a flash, your camera will take a slightly longer time than usual to take a picture, so you will need to keep it especially still. Rest it on something solid (like a wall) or use a tripod if you have one.

● When you are choosing where to stand to take your photograph, try to find a place where there is an interesting silhouette in the foreground – such as a roof, a beach umbrella, or a spiky-looking tree. The black of the silhouette will act as a contrast to the beautiful glowing colours of the sunset, and it will make your photograph a lot more dramatic.

43

photograph water

Water is always fun to photograph, because you never know quite what's going to happen or how it will show up in the shot. Ask your friends over for water games in the garden and you're bound to get some great shots.

Ask some friends to come over and play with spraying water (make sure they don't mind getting wet!). As they are messing around, capture the fun and excitement with your camera. Be sure to stand with the sun in front of you, so that the sunlight shines through the water and makes it sparkle. This will make sure that every single droplet of water stands out in your photos.

Water is much more visible in photos when the sunlight hits it, so always stand facing the sun.

44

play with snow

Snow is always a fun thing to be in and around, especially with lots of friends and a camera.

● The next time you are around snow, either at home or on holiday, take some time out from playing in it to get some really interesting photographs. Snow reflects light, so it creates very vivid areas of brightness and some surprising shadows in landscapes.

● Go out with your camera and ask your friends along to have a snowball fight, go sledging or build a snowman.

● As your friends are playing, capture snowballs flying through the air, sledges whizzing past, or friends gathering snow for a snowman's body.

● When you are photographing people in the snow, remember that because the snow is so brilliantly white, it can tend to make clothes and other objects (like trees) look very dark in contrast. To overcome this, stand with the sun behind you or use the flash on your camera to brighten up the rest of the photograph.

**

make a treasure hunt

This game is fun to make and all your friends will enjoy playing it. Give yourself a whole day to make the map.

● Go for a walk with an adult along a route that you and your friends know quite well, such as the walk to school.

● As you are walking, take photographs of some of the more unusual or stand-out objects along the way. These are the things that you will show on your picture-map to guide your friends on the treasure hunt. Choose some that are easy to spot and others that are harder to find.

● At the end of the route, hide something for your friends to find; this could be an old toy or part of a game. When they find it, you could exchange it for real treasure (like a lollipop!).

● Print the photographs you want to use for the treasure hunt onto an A4 piece of paper, following the same order that these items appear along the route.

● When you are ready to do the treasure hunt, ask an adult to accompany you all on the walk. Give the maps to your friends and explain that they need to find the clues in order. Start everyone off together. When you reach the end of the route, the first person to find the treasure is the winner.

46

find the world in a puddle

Go out with your camera just after it has been raining and find some puddles. Photograph what you see reflected in them.

● Look into the puddles from different angles and heights. The things reflected in them will change as you move around.

● Try photographing the reflections of buildings, plants and trees, or something smaller, like a football.

● Once you have taken your photograph try making ripples in the water and photograph what happens to the reflection.

5

camera tricks

hold up a monument

**

You can turn your friend into a giant by making it look as though he or she is holding up a monument or building using just one hand. This trick uses perspective to make things and people seem smaller or larger than they are.

● Ask a friend to stand in front of a faraway building or a few metres from a park monument and raise one hand as though holding something up with their fingers.

● Now get into position a few metres in front of your friend and look through the camera lens. Direct your friend (saying 'left', 'right' and so on) to move around until it looks as though he or she is touching and holding the top of your chosen building or monument. This position will only look right through the viewfinder of the camera.

● When everything is lined up, take your photograph.

jump on my hand!

Turn your friend into a miniature person, who can stand on a hand and jump up and down on its palm. This is another project that uses perspective to create a trick shot, but this time it makes the person look smaller.

● Ask one of your friends to hold up a hand, palm facing upwards, near your camera. The closer the hand is to the camera the bigger it will appear in the photograph.

● Ask another friend to stand a few metres away from you (preferably on a little hill or mound, so they are already higher than you and the person holding open their hand). You need the hand and person to line up, so direct people until they are in the perfect positions.

● Ask the 'little person' to jump, and take your shot mid-air.

prove that fairies exist

This trick will turn one of your friends into a beautiful flower fairy, dressed in real flower petals.

● Find a flower that looks a little bit like a dress when you turn it upside down, such as a rose or a tulip. Ask your parents for permission to use the flower, and to help you with this trick.

● Ask a girl friend to stand about 3 m (10 ft) away from you.

● Ask your parent to hold the flower near the camera, and to move the flower back and forward until it 'covers' your friend like a skirt. Ask your friend to pose like a dancer so she looks like a dancing fairy, and when everything looks perfect, take a photo.

✳✳

giant toy attack!

Have some fun with one of your toys by making it look as though it is huge and chasing your friends or parents. This time you need the people to look about the same size as the other object (in this case, a toy).

● For this project, the toy will need to be very close to the camera so that it appears big when you look through the lens.

● The people in the photo need to be much further away, so that they appear smaller.

● Lie down on the ground just behind your toy and look through the camera.

● Direct the people until they are in the perfect position to look under attack from the toy, which should look about as big as them. Ask them to look scared, then take the shot.

sky painting

This trick makes it look as though someone is painting the clouds onto the sky. You can do this trick by yourself.

● On a sunny day, when there are just a few drifts of clouds in the sky, go outside with your camera and a paintbrush. Find a cloudstream that you want to 'paint' – it needs to be about the same width as the brush when you look at them both through your camera (vapour trails from planes are good). If the brush looks a bit too big, move it further away from the camera. If it looks too small, move it closer to the camera.

● Make sure the sun is behind you, as this will make the clouds stand out against the sky and make the sky seem even more blue. When you have got the brush and the cloud perfectly aligned through the viewfinder, take the photo.

***

pick up a person

Have you ever thought what it might be like to be able to dangle a little person from your hand? This project lets you show two people in two very different sizes.

If possible, find an outdoor area where there are hardly any objects (like trees) that will give away how you have made this photo. Then ask your parents (or two friends) to stand at different distances from you: one quite close, and the other much further away. Ask the closer one to hold out an arm as though picking something up, and the more distant person to put both hands in the air. Line them up, then take the photo.

The person closest to you should stand so that their whole body fills the camera screen, to make sure they look really tall.

give flowers to a shadow

This is a spooky project – it looks as though someone is playing with a shadow person. Shadows are brilliant for creating 'ghostly' photographs.

● The first thing to remember is that you create a shadow by having the sun behind you.

● Find a fence (or wall) with nothing in front of it, and ask a friend to stand nearby, so their shadow is cast onto the fence. Ask them to raise one hand, as though accepting something, and then get another friend to hold out something (like a flower or toy) to the shadow hand.

● Make sure your shadow is not cast on the fence too, or it will appear in the photograph.

get eaten by a bucket!

**

If you love disaster movies, you'll really like this trick. You're going to photograph a huge bucket descending from the sky and eating all your friends. You could take lots of shots and make a flicker movie (see page 17).

● Ask someone to hold a bucket close to your camera so that it appears very big on your screen.

● Direct some friends to stand a few metres away, but in line with the bucket, so they appear (in your viewfinder) to be underneath it.

● When they are in the right position, ask them to look up and scared, with their arms in the air. Take lots of photos as your other friend very slowly lowers the bucket over their bodies.

55 cloudy ice cream

This project tells you how to photograph a magical ice cream made out of fluffy cloud.

***

● On a sunny day when there are wisps of cloud in the sky, see if you can find a cloud that is quite small and almost circular.

● Looking through your camera towards the sky, ask a friend to hold up an ice-cream cone about 1 m (3 ft) away from you. Tell them to move it up, down, left or right until the cone lines up perfectly with the cloud. You might need to kneel on the ground, so that your friend stands above you.

● When the cloud fits, take the photo of your cloud ice cream.

find the vanishing point ✳

Some things around you – such as paths, passages and train tracks – run in parallel lines. But if you photograph them going into the distance, they join up and disappear!

As things get further away from us they seem smaller and closer together. When parallel lines reach far into the distance, they get so small and close that they join together in one small point, called the 'vanishing point'. The best way to see this is to take a photo of something that runs in lines away from you, like a path going into the distance. You could also try taking a photo of railway tracks, by standing on a bridge above them. Make sure that you use the neck strap or wrist strap on the camera if you are on a bridge, so that you can't accidentally drop the camera.

6

action shots

57

✸✸ one, two, three, jump!

One great way to practise your timing with a camera is to photograph people jumping.

● It can be difficult to get the hang of exactly when to take a photograph, especially when you are shooting moving objects. This is a great way to get to know exactly how quickly the camera responds, and learn when to click and take a shot.

● Ask some friends or siblings to join hands outside somewhere, then to jump in the air when you say so. Stand far enough away from them so that you can see them all in shot, and make sure you keep your camera still. Check that the horizon (the line where the ground meets the sky) appears straight in the photograph, so the ground is a straight line below the jumpers.

58

***

all move together

Roundabouts are a great way to take a photograph that's all about speed, but has very sharp focus.

Sit opposite your friend on a park roundabout and start it spinning so that you are both going round and round. Have your camera ready and photograph your friend while the roundabout is moving. Focus on your friend and take the picture. The faster you go the more blurred the background will be, but your friend will always be in focus.

shoot from the ground

**

This is another great way to photograph action and get really great pictures of your friends against the sky.

Go into the garden or park with your friends and take your camera with you. Lie on your back on the ground, hold your camera so it is pointing directly upwards towards the sky, and ask one of your friends to jump over you. Photograph them as they leap across you – you'll get some really dramatic and interesting pictures that capture all the energy.

friends at fun angles

Go to the park with your friends and photograph them having fun on the slides, swings and climbing frames.

● The trick here is to act like a newspaper reporter. Follow your friends as they take turns on all the activities in the park, and try to choose unusual angles to make your photographs more exciting.

● Plan how you are going to take the photos. Where can you get up high? (Try the climbing frame.) Where would it be good to shoot from low on the ground? (The bottom of a slide is often a great place to sit and shoot.)

● Photograph your friends as they are moving, and as they hesitate before moving. Photograph just their face, or their whole body in action. Experiment! If you want, you could go on the swing, slide or climbing frame yourself to get a very different kind of view and angle. Try sitting or lying on the floor to take the photos – this will instantly make everything appear taller.

61

*** ## low-down, fast-paced

Go to your local skateboard park and capture a real sense of the action by shooting from the ground up.

● You can often get the most dynamic photos of people in action by positioning yourself low on the ground.

● Go to a local skate park with friends and take some time watching whereabouts they go. Decide on the best place to take your photograph from.

● Make sure that you are not in the path of any skaters, and then get as low as you can – kneel or even lie down to take your shots.

● Try using the zoom on the camera to fill the frame with the person skate-jumping.

action and context

A great action shot is all about finding the best angle, so the person with the camera has to move around almost as much as the person being photographed!

✳✳

Find a good location to photograph people doing exciting, sporty things, such as a ski slope or basketball court. If you are photographing friends, tell them whereabouts to go, so that you can get the best shot. Choose your angle carefully, notice what will be in the background, and experiment with using the zoom. Take lots of pictures as the people whizz past you – you never know which shot will really capture the action.

Take a few shots very quickly as they finish – a second, quick shot here caught the winner's joy completely.

get the winning shot

Be a sports photographer for the day and see if you can take a picture that really says "I won!"

● Ask some friends to play in your garden or the park, and organise a mini sports day for them. Mark out the finishing line for a running race and position yourself so that you can photograph the winners coming across the line.

● As they run towards the finishing line, try to photograph the winner crossing the line with their arms in the air, looking really excited. Use your zoom so you can get in close to the racers. Ask them to race a few times, so you can experiment with positions.

7 fun ways

to use photos

64

frame it

It is really satisfying to see your photographs in frames on the wall, perhaps alongside other family photos.

Look for interesting frames at car-boot sales and in charity shops, and ask your parents and grandparents if they have any old frames you can use. You might need to ask an adult to help you fit the photos into the frames and hang them for you. Different shapes, sizes and colour of frames look good together.

put on an exhibition

✳✳✳

Now that you have tons of photos from all the projects you have done, you will want to show off your work to friends and family. Why not put on an exhibition?

Most exhibitions have a theme, so decide on your theme (such as 'friends' or 'tricks') and then look through your photo collection for the best shots. If you have collected some old frames, use these. If you don't have any frames, ask your parents if there is a wall that you can put up photos on using sticky putty (like Blu-Tack®). Then invite lots of people to admire your work – you could even make cards using your photos (see page 116) to use as invitations.

66

* ## make a personalised card

Parents and grandparents love receiving homemade cards. Why not make them a special card using one of your photos, picturing something they really love?

● Choose a photograph that you think really suits the person who will be receiving the card. If your mum loves roses, for instance, you could use a photo of a bunch of roses.

● Ask someone to print out the photo on special photo paper, then get a piece of A4 card, fold it in half, and stick the photo onto the front. Add a message to the inside and put one on the front too, if you like.

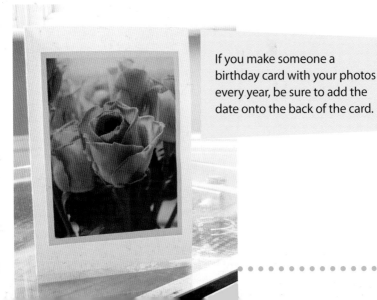

If you make someone a birthday card with your photos every year, be sure to add the date onto the back of the card.

**

make a calendar

Making a calendar of your photos is a perfect way to show your new skills and it makes a perfect Christmas present for your family and friends.

● Look back through all your photos and select 12 to put in the calendar. You will need one for each month, and it works best if the photos reflect the right time of year; so use sunny, summery ones for June, July and August, for instance.

● Find a company that makes personalised calendars (there are lots to choose from on the internet). Or you could make one yourself, by sticking your selected photographs onto card and drawing up a very personalised calendar.

use a digital frame

Another great way to view all the photographs you have taken and to share them with everyone else is to put them onto a digital frame.

A digital photo frame is a special frame that acts a bit like a computer screen. If you put the memory card from your camera into the side of the frame, the pictures you have taken will show on the screen one after another as a slide show. After you have given the frame to someone, you can also send them new pictures over the internet – they can download them straight onto the frame and watch them. This is a great way to keep grandparents up-to-date with what you are doing.

make a collage

Every picture tells a story, but a collection of pictures can tell an even bigger story – of your holidays, school term, or even a whole year. Why not make a collage of pictures on a piece of card, then hang it on your bedroom wall?

● You will need a piece of card, some photos that you have chosen, scissors and some glue.

● Put all the photographs onto the card and see which ones look good next to each other. They don't all need to be in a neat straight line – overlap some of them and put some at different angles to one another. When you are happy with your arrangement, glue the photos into place.

Choose a mixture of close-up and distance shots so that your collage has lots of variation and some large areas of colour.

70

your life in pictures

Some people write diaries, but photographers like to make photographic diaries, recording their lives in pictures. This is a project you could carry on with forever!

- Once a week or so, look through your pictures from the week and choose some that will remind you of how you spent your time. They might show you playing your favourite sport, or messing around with friends, or they might be pictures of other people that you have spent time with. They might show some of your favourite places, or favourite food. Choose anything that feels really important to you right now.

- To make the journal, you can use a notebook or a diary. Stick the photos you have chosen into the journal, and write beside them any details you want to remember, like who is in the photo, and when it was taken.

- Try to keep your camera with you often during the week, so you can photograph all the special moments and fun times you have with your friends and family.

camera stuff

If you enjoy playing with a camera, you will soon want to experiment with all its special buttons. This is a guide to the most important ones, and will tell you how to use them.

The 'Auto' setting

This is the setting that most people use, pretty much all the time. When the camera is set to this mode, it will decide automatically how much light to let in, how slowly or quickly to take the photo, and whether or not to use the flash. In Auto mode, your flash will automatically come on when there isn't enough light for your photograph, but don't be afraid to turn your flash off in some cases.

The 'Night' setting

Use this setting when you are photographing at night but want to keep the atmospheric light that is around you, rather than lose it by using a bright flash. The Night setting automatically slows down the shutter speed to allow the ambient light to record on the camera, but this means you do need to keep the camera very still, or you will get a blurred photo.

Common camera symbols

Landscape ▣

Night portrait ♠ˀ

Self-timer ⟳

Close up/Macro ❀

The 'Self-timer' setting

If you use this setting and press the shutter button (the button you click to take a photo), you will have about 10 seconds before the camera takes the photo. This means that if you want to get into the shot yourself, you can set the self-timer, push the shutter button, and run into place in time for the photo. Some cameras have a flashing light to let you know when the camera will take the photo, while others have a 'beep'.

The 'Close-up' or 'Macro' setting

This lets you focus on a small object really close to your camera lens and get it in perfect focus. Some cameras will let you focus less than an inch from the object; with others it may be a little further away.

The 'Portrait' setting

Use the Portrait setting when you are taking a portrait of someone. A good portrait focuses on the person, and has few distractions in the background. The Portrait mode does this for you – it will automatically set the camera to have a narrow depth of field, which means that it makes the person in the portrait crisply in focus, and the background softly out of focus.

The 'Landscape' setting

The Landscape mode on your camera automatically sets the camera's focus to infinity. This means you can take wide shots of your favourite landscapes (buildings, beaches and so on) and everything in the image will be sharply in focus.

index

acknowledgments

Thank you to Becs and Zac for all your love, inspiration and support.

Thanks also to all the excellent models who helped with the projects in the book: Max, Bruno, Ella and Otto Moore, Cameron Daitz, Isha Clarke, Jessica Prebble, Samuel Prebble, Isla Kerr, Ben Leighton, Finlay Leighton, Tamsin Orford-Williams, Jennifer Orford-Williams, Zeki Jones, Christina Murunai, Mia Cobbold, Jack Cobbold, Zac Davis, Whinnie, Humphrey and Monty the dog.

Tracy and Sarah, thanks for all your encouragement and belief, and for always being at the end of the phone day or night.

Thank you to everyone who picks up a camera and sees the world in a new light.

Produced for Frances Lincoln by Tracy Killick Art Direction and Design and www.editorsonline.org

Commissioning Editor: Sarah Tomley
Art Director: Tracy Killick
Photography by: John Davis with help from Bruno Moore, Max Moore, Cameron Daitz, David Foster, Tamsin Orford-Williams, Jennifer Orford-Williams, Jessica Prebble
Proofreader: Louise Abbott